BEANSTALK'S BASICS FOR
PIANO
THEORY BOOK
PREPARATORY LEVEL B

BY CHERYL FINN

WILLIS MUSIC

12297

CONTENTS

A NOTE TO PARENTS AND TEACHERS

The study of music theory is essential to the development of the young musician. Not only does this study help to expand upon the concepts taught at the piano lesson, but it also gives the student a greater understanding and appreciation of the wonder that is music.

Beanstalk's Basics for Piano Theory uses colorful and attractive stickers to reward a job well done. The student receives stickers for note naming and note writing drills, for ear training and sight reading exercises and for successfully completing review pages. As with the lesson book, we recommend that the teacher remove the sticker sheet as the student begins each book. This preserves the element of surprise and increases motivation.

Each theory page corresponds directly with material covered in ***Beanstalk's Basics for Piano***. The student progresses gradually, in a logical fashion and continually builds on concepts previously learned.

Beanstalk's Basics for Piano Theory also features a further learning tool called ***Thinking Cap***. ***Thinking Cap*** challenges the student to search for answers to one or more theoretical questions and to provide these answers verbally as part of a musical dialogue. This fun exercise encourages students to carefully consider and discuss new concepts as they arise.

We wish much success to all students as they strive to expand their musical horizons!

To Alanna and Brianne

12297

INTERVALS

An **INTERVAL** is the distance between **TWO** notes.

2nd

The distance from one white key to the next white key - above or below - is a **2nd**.

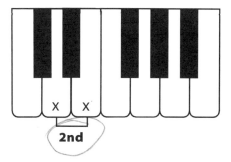

1. For each key named below, name the key which is a **2nd HIGHER**.

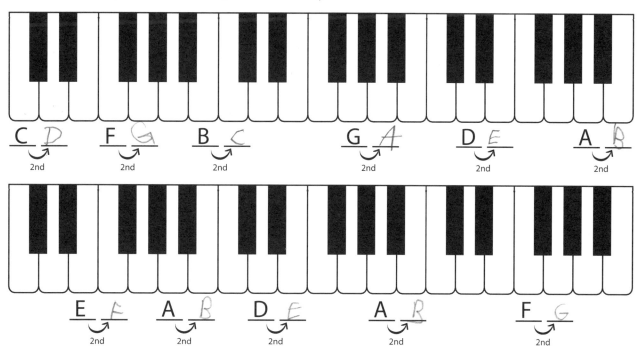

C D   F G   B C   G A   D E   A B
2nd   2nd   2nd   2nd   2nd   2nd

E F   A B   D E   A B   F G
2nd   2nd   2nd   2nd   2nd

2. For each key named below, name the key which is a **2nd LOWER**.

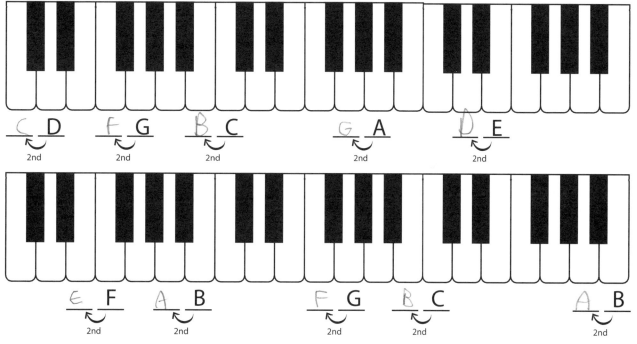

C D   F G   B C   G A   D E
2nd   2nd   2nd   2nd   2nd

E F   A B   F G   B C   A B
2nd   2nd   2nd   2nd   2nd

CORRESPONDS WITH PAGES 3 AND 4 OF BEANSTALK'S LESSON PREP B.

ARE THESE 2NDS GOING UP OR DOWN?

1. Each measure below contains an interval of a **2nd**. Draw an arrow above each **2nd** to show if the interval is going up (↗) or going down (↘).

2. Name the notes.

NOW HEAR THIS!

Your teacher will play a series of **2nds** twice. Close your eyes and listen. Are the **2nds** a step **HIGHER** or a step **LOWER**?

FOR THE TEACHER:

CORRESPONDS WITH PAGE 5 OF BEANSTALK'S LESSON PREP B.

12297

INTERVALS

How can you tell the
difference between a
2nd and a *3rd*?

3rd

When there is a skip of **ONE** white
key on the keyboard the interval
is called a *3rd*.

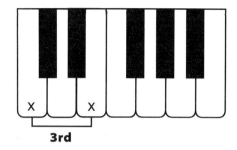

1. For each key named below, name the key which is a *3rd HIGHER*.

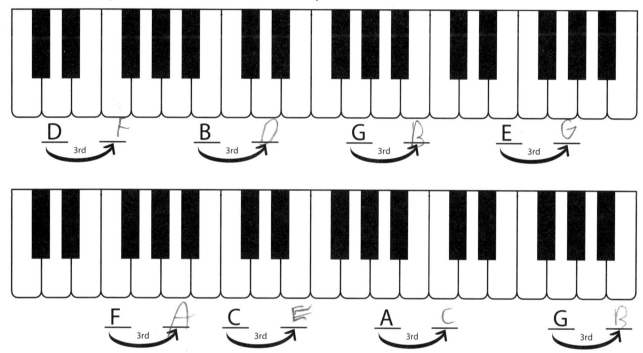

2. For each key named below, name the key which is a *3rd LOWER*.

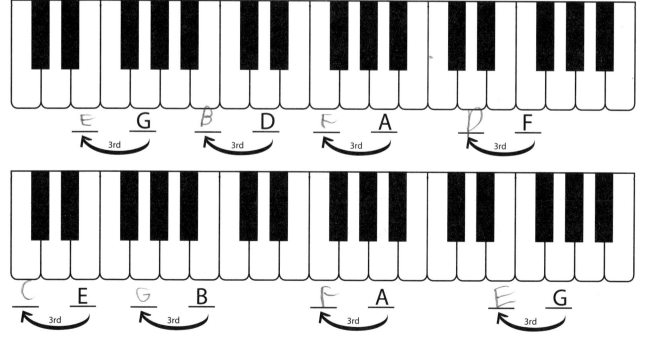

CORRESPONDS WITH PAGES 6 AND 7 OF BEANSTALK'S LESSON PREP B.

12297

5

ARE THESE 3RDS GOING UP OR DOWN?

1. Each measure below contains an interval of a **3rd**. Draw an arrow above each **3rd** to show if the interval is going up (↗) or going down (↘).

2. Name the notes.

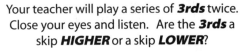

NOW HEAR THIS!

Your teacher will play a series of **3rds** twice. Close your eyes and listen. Are the **3rds** a skip **HIGHER** or a skip **LOWER**?

FOR THE TEACHER:

CORRESPONDS WITH PAGE 8 OF BEANSTALK'S LESSON PREP B.

12297

INTERVALS

THINKING CAP

How can you tell the difference between a *3rd* and a *4th*?

4TH

When there is a skip of *TWO* white keys on the keyboard the interval is called a *4th*.

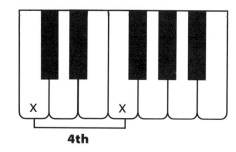

1. For each key named below, name the key which is a *4th HIGHER*.

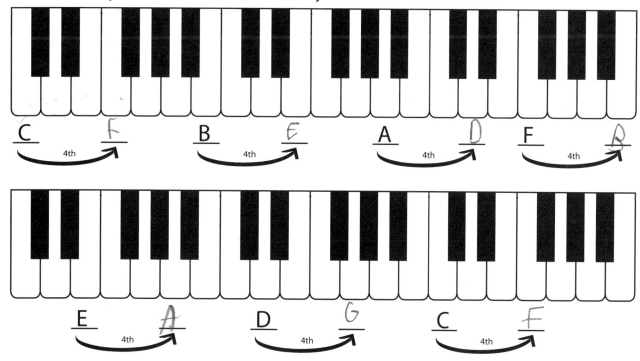

C — F   B — E   A — D   F — B

E — A   D — G   C — F

2. For each key named below, name the key which is a *4th LOWER*.

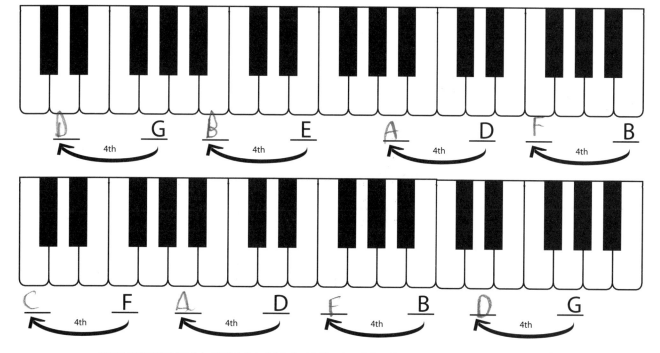

D — G   B — E   A — D   F — B

C — F   A — D   F — B   D — G

CORRESPONDS WITH PAGES 9 AND 10 OF BEANSTALK'S LESSON PREP B.

ARE THESE 4THS GOING UP OR DOWN?

1. Each measure below contains an interval of a **4th**. Draw an arrow above each **4th** to show if the interval is going up (↗) or going down (↘).

2. Name the notes.

CORRESPONDS WITH PAGE 11 OF BEANSTALK'S LESSON PREP B.

12297

INTERVALS

THINKING CAP

How can you tell the difference between a *4th* and a *5th*?

5TH

When there is a skip of *THREE* white keys on the keyboard the interval is called a *5th*.

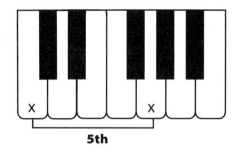

1. For each key named below, name the key which is a *5th HIGHER*.

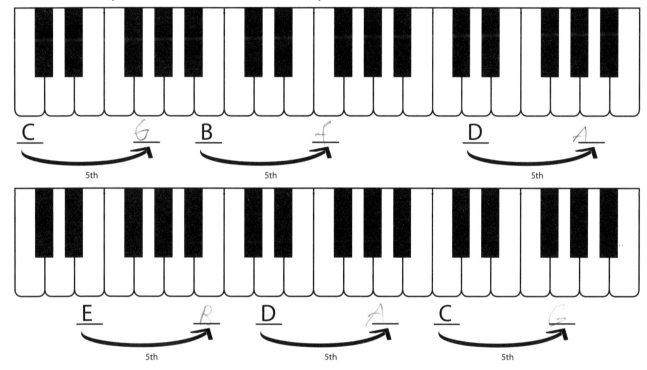

C → G   B → F   D → A

E → B   D → A   C → G

2. For each key named below, name the key which is a *5th LOWER*.

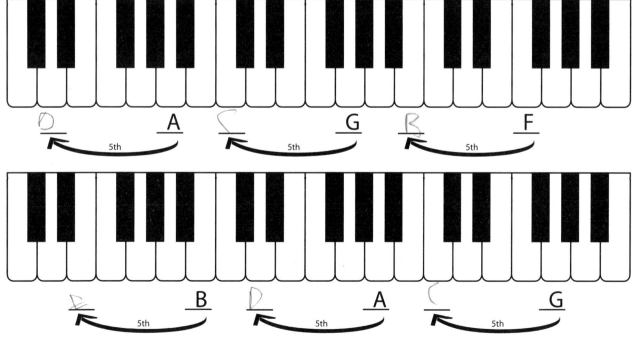

D ← A   C ← G   B ← F

E ← B   D ← A   C ← G

CORRESPONDS WITH PAGE 12 OF BEANSTALK'S LESSON PREP B.

ARE THESE 5THS GOING UP OR DOWN?

1. Each measure below contains an **INTERVAL** of a **5th**. Draw an arrow above each **5th** to show if the interval is going up (↗) or going down (↘).

2. Name the notes.

HARMONIC & MELODIC

There are **TWO** kinds of intervals, **HARMONIC** and **MELODIC**.

An interval is **HARMONIC** if the notes are written **ON TOP** of each other and are played at the **SAME TIME**.

An interval is **MELODIC** if the notes are written **BESIDE** each other and are played **SEPARATELY**.

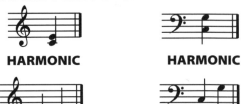

1. Draw a **CIRCLE** around each **HARMONIC** interval.

2. Draw a **BOX** around each **MELODIC** interval.

3. Name the interval distance.

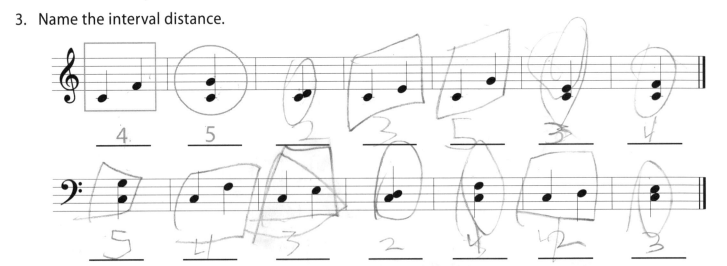

NOW HEAR THIS!

Your teacher will play some **INTERVALS** twice. Close your eyes and listen. Is the interval **HARMONIC** or **MELODIC**?

FOR THE TEACHER:

CORRESPONDS WITH PAGE 13 OF BEANSTALK'S LESSON PREP B.

12297

STACCATO

THINKING CAP

What is the difference in sound between a *STACCATO* and a *SLUR*?

A dot written **ABOVE** or **BELOW** a note means that the note is to be played with a **STACCATO** touch. **STACCATO** tells us to play **DETACHED** or **CRISPLY**.

1. Add **STACCATO DOTS** to all the notes below. (If the note stem is going **UP** (♩) the dot goes **BELOW** the note. If the note stem is going **DOWN** (♩) the dot goes **ABOVE** the note.)

2. Play the melody as written. (Did you remember to play crisply?)

3. Name the notes.

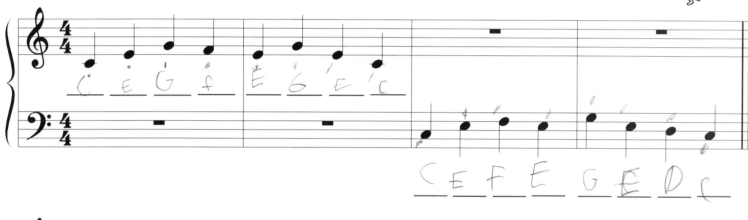

NOW HEAR THIS!

Your teacher will play a series of notes. Close your eyes and listen. Are the notes you are hearing played **STACCATO** or **LEGATO**?

FOR THE TEACHER:

CORRESPONDS WITH PAGE 14 OF BEANSTALK'S LESSON PREP B.

COUNTING

THINKING CAP

How many counts will
there be in each measure of $\frac{3}{4}$?

Write the counts for the following.

CORRESPONDS WITH PAGE 15 OF BEANSTALK'S LESSON PREP B.

12297

PUZZLE FUN!

 TREASURE HUNT

1. Find **TWO QUARTER NOTES** and circle them in **BLUE**.

2. Find **THREE HALF RESTS** and circle them in **GREEN**.

3. Find **TWO WHOLE NOTES** and circle them in **ORANGE**.

4. Find **ONE QUARTER REST** and circle it in **RED**.

5. Find **TWO HALF NOTES** and circle them in **PURPLE**.

6. Find **ONE WHOLE REST** and circle it in **BROWN**.

7. Find **THREE DOTTED HALF NOTES** and circle them in **YELLOW**.

 NOW HEAR THIS!

Your teacher will play a series of notes in $\frac{3}{4}$ time. Close your eyes and listen. After hearing them played twice, **CLAP** back the rhythm you heard!

 **FOR THE TEACHER:**

CORRESPONDS WITH PAGE 16 OF BEANSTALK'S LESSON PREP B.

ONCE UPON A TIME ...

LUDWIG VAN BEETHOVEN was born in 1770 in Bonn, Germany. He came from a very musical family. His father and grandfather were both singers for the local prince. Beethoven was only eleven years old when he was asked by the prince to be the assistant organist at the court chapel. When he was twelve years old he joined the court orchestra as a harpsichordist.

At the age of seventeen, Beethoven was introduced to the great composer Mozart. Mozart was very impressed with Beethoven's playing as were the prince and many counts who heard him play. They loved his music and they rewarded him with many gifts.

When Beethoven was in his late twenties, tragedy struck. He began to go deaf. He continued to compose, writing symphonies, piano sonatas, violin sonatas, string quartets and even one opera called *Fidelio*.

In 1827, when he was 57 years old, he became ill and died. Beethoven is one of the world's greatest and most famous composers. Even though he lived 200 years ago, we still hear and love his music to this day.

Answer the following questions about Beethoven:

1. How many years ago did Beethoven live? _____241 years_____

2. For whom did Beethoven's father and grandfather sing? _the local prince_

3. How old was Beethoven when he began to play the organ at the court chapel? _11_

4. Who did Beethoven meet when he was seventeen years old? _Mozart_

5. What began to happen to Beethoven when he was in his late twenties? _He began_
    to go deaf

6. How old was Beethoven when he died? _fifty-seven_

NOTE NAMING
3 NEW NOTES IN THE BASS CLEF!

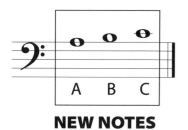

NEW NOTES

Name the following whole notes in the **BASS CLEF**.

CORRESPONDS WITH PAGE 18 OF BEANSTALK'S LESSON PREP B.

MORE NOTE NAMING!

Time yourself naming the following whole notes. (Remember to check the **CLEFS**!)

I named these notes in ___4___ minutes and ___50___ seconds!

CORRESPONDS WITH PAGE 19 OF BEANSTALK'S LESSON PREP B.

12297

REVIEW

1. Name the following **INTERVALS**. Put a **BOX** around all of the **HARMONIC INTERVALS**. Put a **CIRCLE** around all of the **MELODIC INTERVALS**.

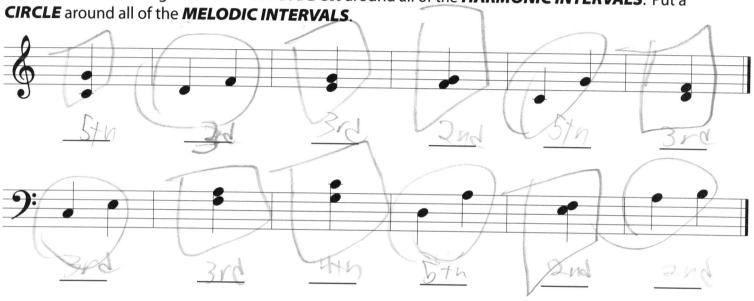

2. Write the **COUNTS** for the following.

CORRESPONDS WITH PAGES 20 AND 21 OF BEANSTALK'S LESSON PREP B.

12297

17

3. Name the following whole notes in the **TREBLE CLEF**.

F   C   G   F   C   E   D

4. Name the following whole notes in the **BASS CLEF**.

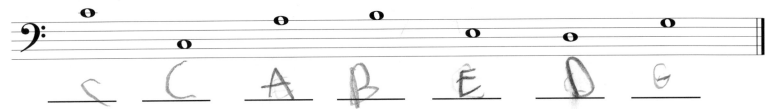

C   C   A   B   E   D   G

5. Add **STACCATOS** to the following notes.

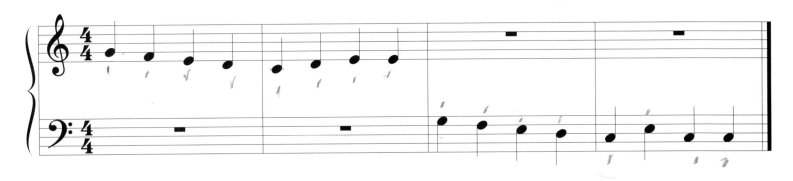

6. Match the following musical signs to their correct meanings.

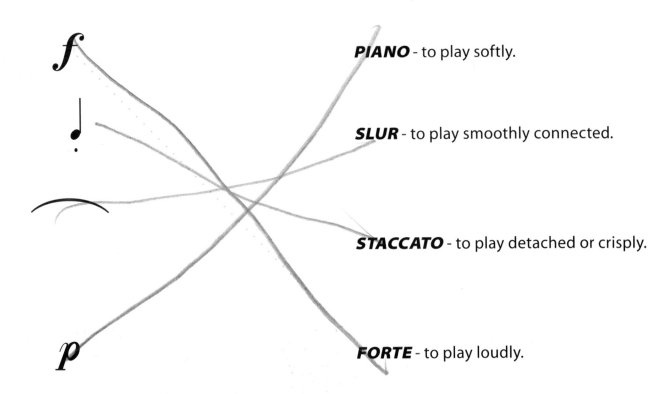

PIANO - to play softly.

SLUR - to play smoothly connected.

STACCATO - to play detached or crisply.

FORTE - to play loudly.

CORRESPONDS WITH PAGES 20 AND 21 OF BEANSTALK'S LESSON PREP B.

18   12297

Do#

COUNTING

THINKING CAP

How many counts will there be in each measure of $\frac{2}{4}$?

Write the counts for the following.

1 2 3   1 2 3   1 2 3   1 2 3

1 2 3 4   1 2 3 4   1 2 3 4   1 2 3 4

1 2   1 2   1 2   1 2

1 2 3   1 2 3   1 2 3   1 2 3

1 2 3 4   1 2 3 4   1 2 3 4   1 2 3 4

**NOW HEAR THIS!**

Your teacher will play a series of notes in $\frac{4}{4}$ time. Close your eyes and listen. After hearing them played twice, **CLAP** back the rhythm you heard!

**FOR THE TEACHER:**

CORRESPONDS WITH PAGE 22 OF BEANSTALK'S LESSON PREP B.

NOTE WRITING

When writing notes it is very important to be neat.

A **LINE** note must be written neatly on the line.　　　　　**NOT**

A **SPACE** note must be written neatly in the space.　　　　**NOT**

For **MIDDLE C**　　do not write the note too high:　　or too low:

Trace the following whole notes on the staff in the **TREBLE CLEF**.

C　　F　　D　　G　　E　　C　　F

Draw the following whole notes on the staff in the **TREBLE CLEF**.

F　　C　　E　　D　　G　　F　　D

Trace the following whole notes on the staff in the **BASS CLEF**.

F　　C　　E　　D　　G　　C　　B

Draw the following whole notes on the staff in the **BASS CLEF**.

D　　F　　B　　C　　G　　E　　A

MORE NOTE WRITING!

Draw the following whole notes on the staff in the **TREBLE CLEF**.

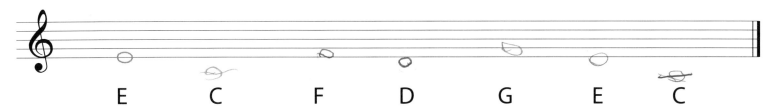

E   C   F   D   G   E   C

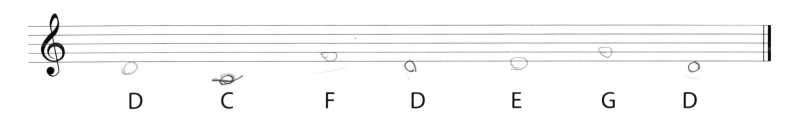

D   C   F   D   E   G   D

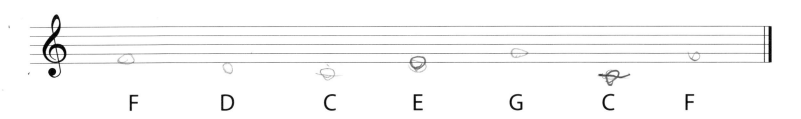

F   D   C   E   G   C   F

Draw the following whole notes on the staff in the **BASS CLEF**.

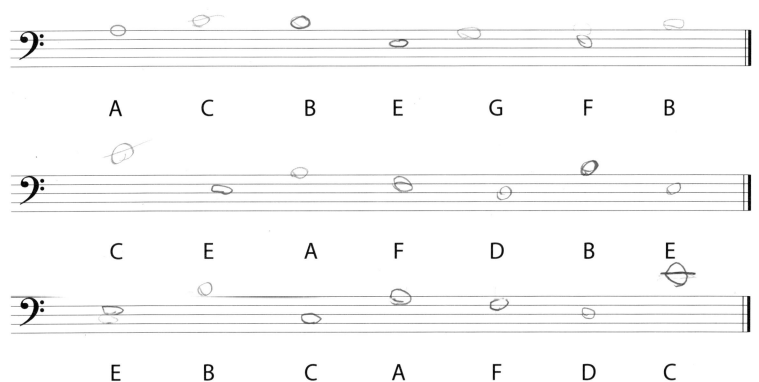

A   C   B   E   G   F   B

C   E   A   F   D   B   E

E   B   C   A   F   D   C

Do 10/14/11

NOTE NAMING
4 NEW NOTES IN THE TREBLE CLEF!

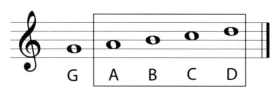

NEW NOTES

Name the following whole notes in the **TREBLE CLEF**.

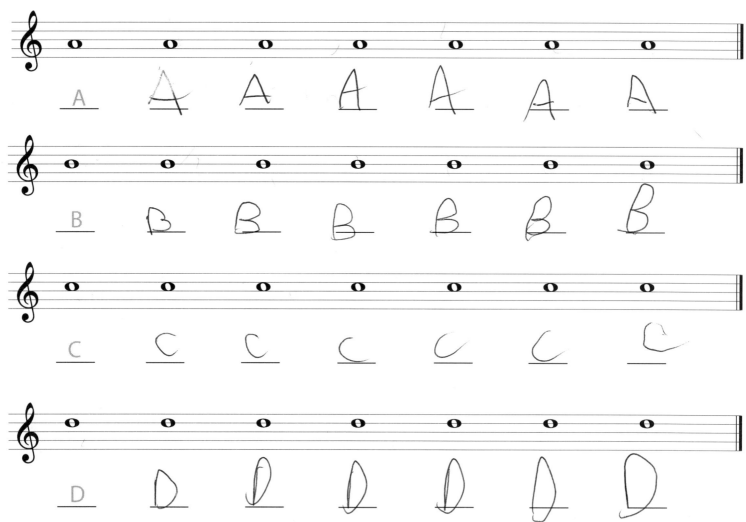

A A A A A A A A

B B B B B B B B

C C C C C C C C

D D D D D D D D

Name the following whole notes in the **TREBLE CLEF**.

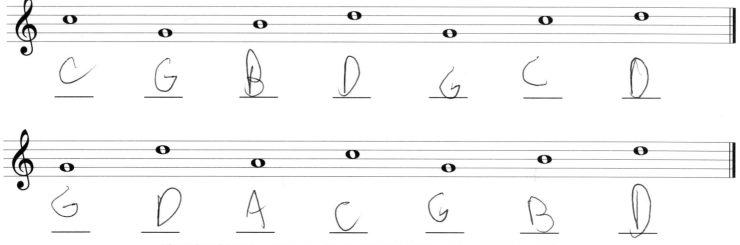

C G B D G C D

G D A C G B D

CORRESPONDS WITH PAGE 25 OF BEANSTALK'S LESSON PREP B.

12297

NOTE NAMING
3 NEW NOTES IN THE BASS CLEF!

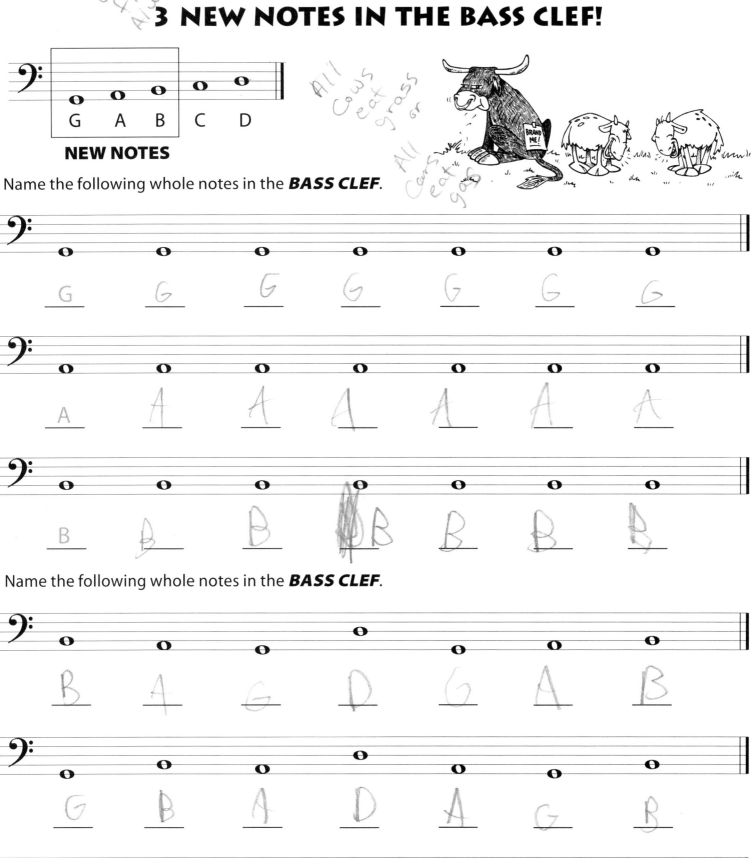

Name the following whole notes in the **BASS CLEF**.

Name the following whole notes in the **BASS CLEF**.

MORE NOTE NAMING!

Time yourself naming the following whole notes in the **TREBLE CLEF**.

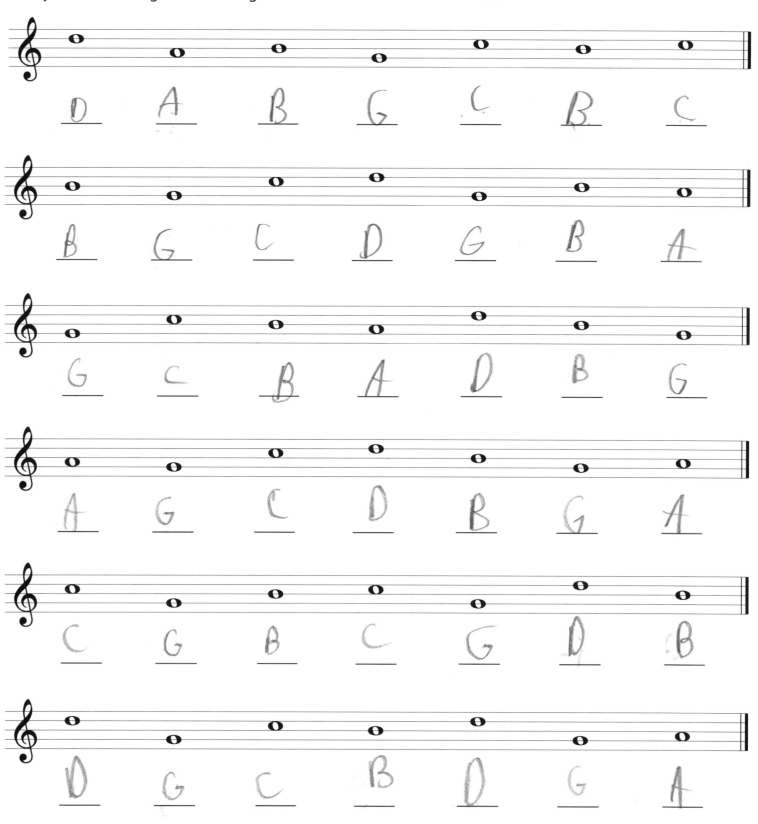

D A B G C B C

B G C D G B A

G C B A D B G

A G C D B G A

C G B C G D B

D G C B D G A

I named these notes in ___1___ minutes and ___49___ seconds!

CORRESPONDS WITH PAGES 27 AND 28 OF BEANSTALK'S LESSON PREP B.

12297

MORE NOTE NAMING!

IT'S NICK!

Time yourself naming the following whole notes in the **BASS CLEF**.

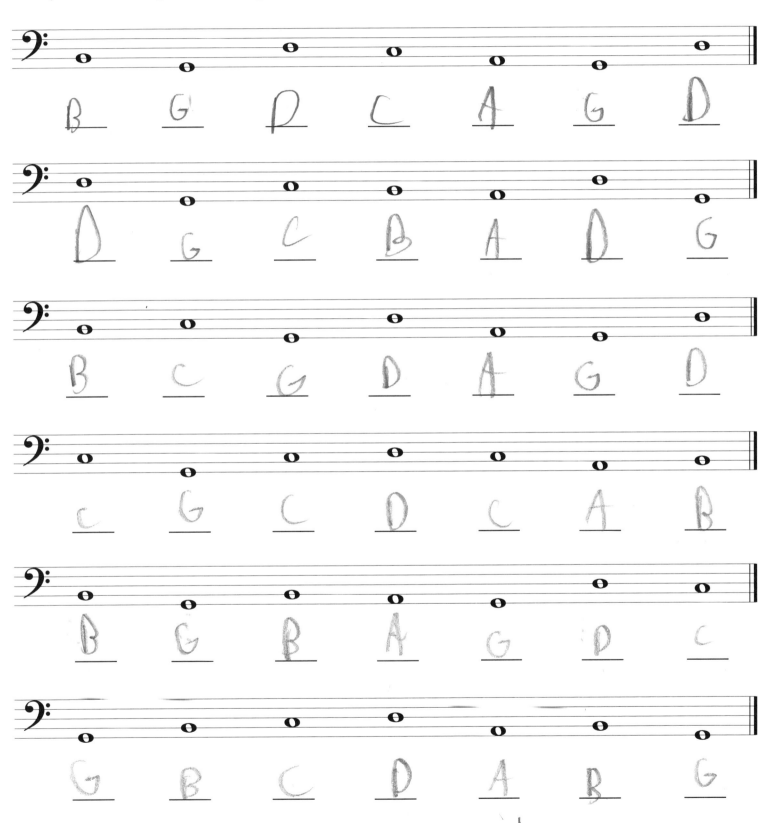

I named these notes in ___1___ minutes and ___53___ seconds!

CORRESPONDS WITH PAGE 29 OF BEANSTALK'S LESSON PREP B.

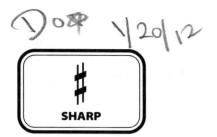

SHARPS

This is a **SHARP** sign: ♯
It tells us to play the closest key to the **RIGHT**, which may be a black or white key.

Trace these **SHARP** signs. (Drawing hint: A **SHARP** sign resembles a tic-tac-toe board.)

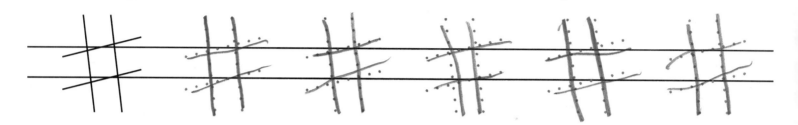

Draw 6 more **SHARP** signs.

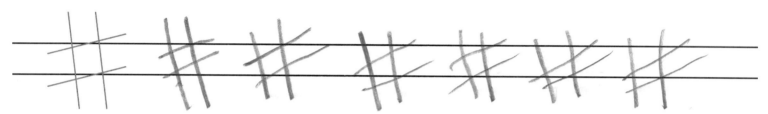

NATURALS

This is a **NATURAL** sign: ♮   A **NATURAL** is used to **CANCEL** a **SHARP**.

Trace these **NATURAL** signs. (Drawing hint: First draw the letter 'L', then the number '7'.)

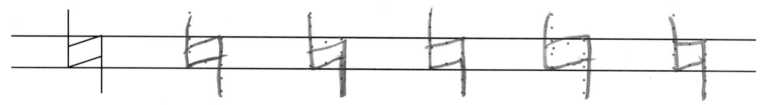

Draw 6 more **NATURAL** signs.

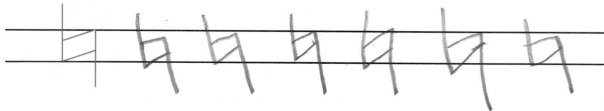

CORRESPONDS WITH PAGES 30 AND 31 OF BEANSTALK'S LESSON PREP B.

Do 1/20/12

COUNTING

THINKING CAP

How many counts will there be in each measure of $\frac{4}{4}$?

Write the counts for the following.

CORRESPONDS WITH PAGES 32 AND 33 OF BEANSTALK'S LESSON PREP B.

12297   27

CRESCENDO

A NEW DYNAMIC SIGN

This is a **CRESCENDO** sign:
CRESCENDO means to play **GRADUALLY LOUDER**.

1. Trace these **CRESCENDO** signs:

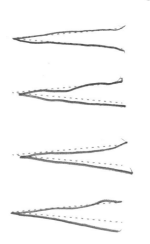

2. Draw 4 more **CRESCENDO** signs below.

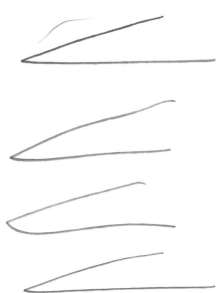

PUZZLE FUN!

Look at each of the musical signs below. If the sign matches the meaning, color the box **BLUE**.
If the sign **DOES NOT** match the meaning, color the box **RED**.

Can you find the
TIC-TAC-TOE?

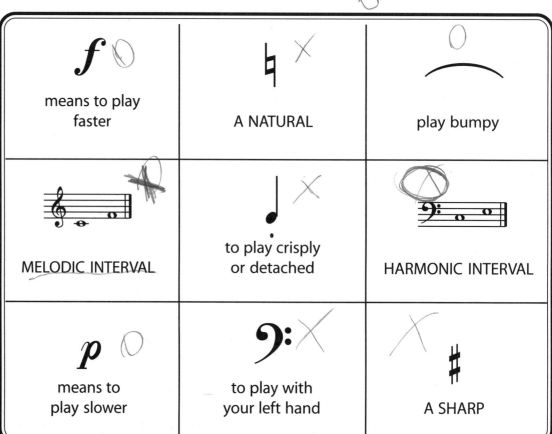

f means to play faster	♮ A NATURAL	play bumpy
MELODIC INTERVAL	to play crisply or detached	HARMONIC INTERVAL
p means to play slower	𝄢 to play with your left hand	♯ A SHARP

CORRESPONDS WITH PAGE 34 OF BEANSTALK'S LESSON PREP B.

12297

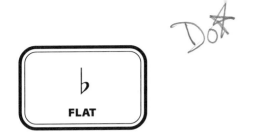

FLAT

FLATS

This is a **FLAT** sign: ♭
It tells us to play the closest key to the **LEFT**, which may be a black or white key.

Trace these **FLAT** signs. (Drawing hint: A **FLAT** sign resembles the letter 'b'.)

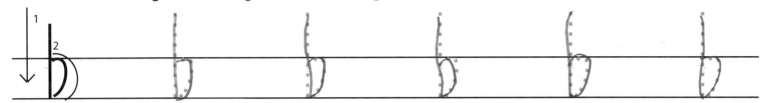

Draw 6 more **FLAT** signs.

Reminder: A **NATURAL** sign is used to cancel a **FLAT** or a **SHARP**.

SHARPS, FLATS & NATURALS

1. Put a **BOX** around all of the **SHARP** signs.
2. Put a **CIRCLE** around all of the **FLAT** signs.
3. Put a **TRIANGLE** around all of the **NATURAL** signs.

THINKING CAP
Which sign is used to cancel the others?

How many **SHARPS** did you find? ___9___   How many **FLATS**? ___8___   How many **NATURALS**? ___7___

CORRESPONDS WITH PAGE 35 OF BEANSTALK'S LESSON PREP B.

A NEW DYNAMIC SIGN

THINKING CAP
How can you tell the difference between a **CRESCENDO** sign and a **DECRESCENDO** sign?

This is a **DECRESCENDO** sign: ▷
DECRESCENDO means to play **GRADUALLY SOFTER**.

1. Trace these **DECRESCENDO** signs:

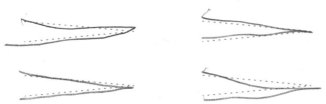

2. Draw 4 more **DECRESCENDO** signs below.

NOW HEAR THIS!

Your teacher will play a series of notes twice. Close your eyes and listen. Are the notes **GETTING LOUDER** or **GETTING SOFTER**? Answer *"crescendo"* or *"decrescendo"*.

FOR THE TEACHER:

? RIDDLES! ?

I am a rest.
I silently sit on the middle line.
Some think I look like a hat.
I get **TWO** counts!

What am I? half rest

Draw me!

I am a sign.
I am very small, just barely a dot.
When I come with a note I make it detached and crisp.

What am I? stecato

Draw me! _____

I am a dynamic sign.
I come from the alphabet.
I make big sounds.
My real name is **FORTE**.

Draw me! f

I am a sign.
I come from the alphabet.
I make small sounds.
My real name is **PIANO**.

Draw me! P

I am a rest.
I hang upside down.
I get all the counts in the bar.

What am I? whole rest

Draw me!

I am a sign.
I make music smooth.
I help to join notes together.
My name rhymes with ' blur.'

What am I? slur

Draw me! ‿‿

CORRESPONDS WITH PAGE 36 OF BEANSTALK'S LESSON PREP B.

NOTE NAMING!

IT'S NICK!

Time yourself naming the following whole notes. Remember to check the **CLEFS**! **HINT**: When naming a **SHARP** or a **FLAT**, the signs comes **AFTER** the letter name of the note. (Examples: F♯, B♭)

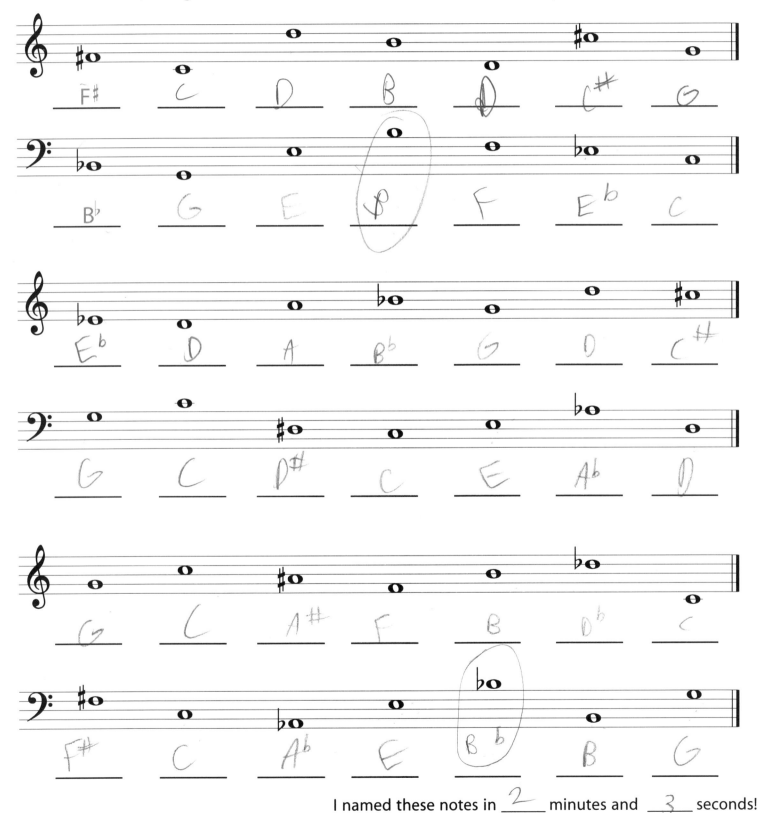

I named these notes in __2__ minutes and __3__ seconds!

CORRESPONDS WITH PAGE 37 OF BEANSTALK'S LESSON PREP B.

THE TIE

A **TIE** joins two notes on the same line or space and means to play the first note and hold for the value of both notes.

Notice how the **TIE** looks quite similar to the **SLUR**!

Reminder: It is a **SLUR** if the notes are **DIFFERENT** from each other. It is a **TIE** if the notes are the **SAME** as each other.

1. Put a **CIRCLE** around all of the **SLURS**.

2. Put a **BOX** around all of the **TIES**.

THINKING CAP
How can you tell the difference between a **SLUR** and a **TIE**?

How many **SLURS** did you find? _7_   How many **TIES** did you find? _5_

NOW HEAR THIS!

Your teacher will play a series of **SLURRED NOTES**. Close your eyes and listen. Are the notes getting **HIGHER** or **LOWER**?

FOR THE TEACHER:

CORRESPONDS WITH PAGES 38 AND 39 OF BEANSTALK'S LESSON PREP B.

12297

MYSTERY WORDS!

Name the following notes and find the *MYSTERY WORDS*!

CORRESPONDS WITH PAGES 38 AND 39 OF BEANSTALK'S LESSON PREP B.

12297

33

INTERVALS

Name the **INTERVAL** distance for the following notes.

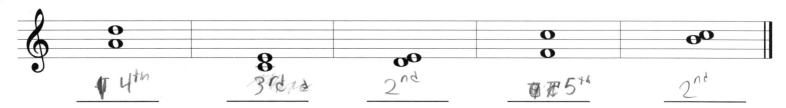

4th   3rd   2nd   5th   2nd

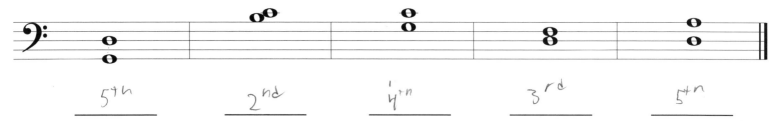

5th   2nd   4th   3rd   5th

THINKING CAP

How do you know if an interval is **HARMONIC**?

HARMONIC OR MELODIC?

For the following **INTERVALS** put a **CIRCLE** around all of the **HARMONIC** intervals and a **BOX** around all of the **MELODIC** intervals.

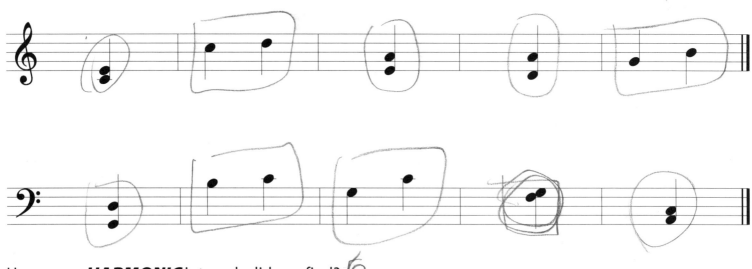

How many **HARMONIC** intervals did you find? 5

How many **MELODIC** intervals did you find? 4

NOW HEAR THIS!

Your teacher will play a series of intervals. Close your eyes and listen. Is the interval **HARMONIC** or **MELODIC**?

FOR THE TEACHER:

CORRESPONDS WITH PAGE 40 OF BEANSTALK'S LESSON PREP B.

12297

NOTE NAMING
& WRITING
(C POSITION REVIEW)

IT'S NICK!

1. Time yourself naming the following whole notes.

I named these notes in 0 minutes and 50 seconds!

2. Time yourself writing the following whole notes.

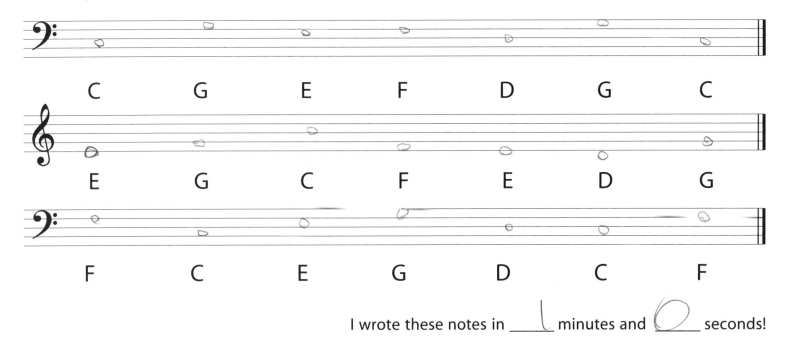

I wrote these notes in 1 minutes and 0 seconds!

CORRESPONDS WITH PAGE 41 OF BEANSTALK'S LESSON PREP B.

NOTE NAMING
& WRITING
(MIDDLE C POSITION REVIEW)

IT'S NICK!

1. Time yourself naming the following whole notes.

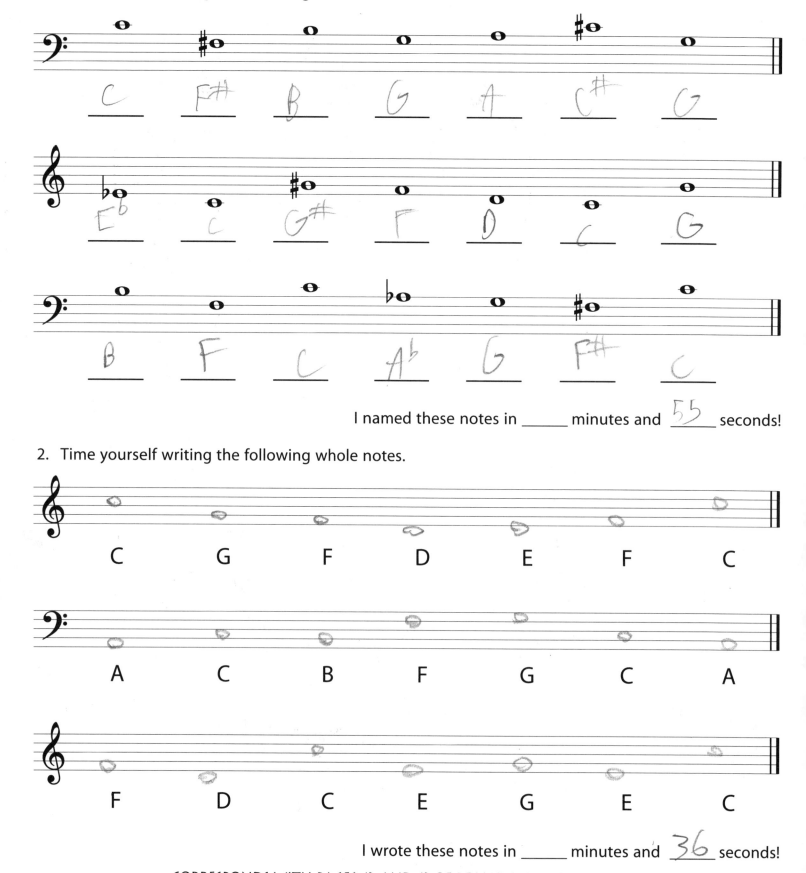

C   F#   B   G   A   C#   G

E♭   C   G#   F   D   C   G

B   F   C   A♭   G   F#   C

I named these notes in _____ minutes and 55 seconds!

2. Time yourself writing the following whole notes.

C   G   F   D   E   F   C

A   C   B   F   G   C   A

F   D   C   E   G   E   C

I wrote these notes in _____ minutes and 36 seconds!

CORRESPONDS WITH PAGES 42 AND 43 OF BEANSTALK'S LESSON PREP B.

12297

NOTE NAMING & WRITING
(G POSITION REVIEW)

IT'S NICK!

1. Time yourself naming the following whole notes.

D   G#   C   A   Bb   D   A

B   G   D   C#   A   D   C

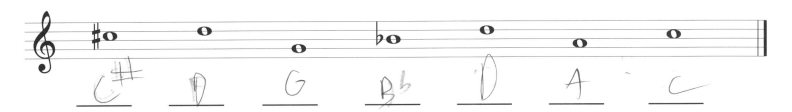

C#   D   G   Bb   D   A   C

I named these notes in _____ minutes and __2__ seconds!

2. Time yourself writing the following whole notes.

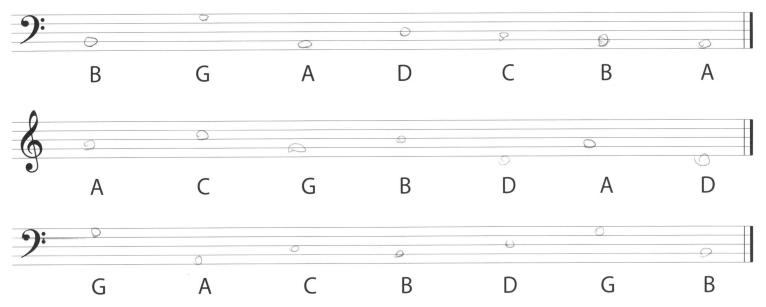

B   G   A   D   C   B   A

A   C   G   B   D   A   D

G   A   C   B   D   G   B

I wrote these notes in _____ minutes and __37__ seconds!

CORRESPONDS WITH PAGES 44 AND 45 OF BEANSTALK'S LESSON PREP B.

PUZZLE FUN!
(YES! OR NO!)

Answer the questions below by putting a **CHECK MARK** (✓)
in the correct box.

YES! **NO!**

1. This is a **WHOLE REST**: ▬   ☐   ☑

2. 𝄞 means to play with your **LEFT HAND**.   ☐   ☑

3. This is a **SLUR**: 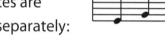 It means to play bumpy.   ☑   ☑

4. 𝄢 means to play with your **RIGHT HAND**.   ☐   ☑

5. A **STACCATO** ˙ means to play detached and crisply.   ☑   ☐

6. This is a **3rd**:   ☑   ☐

7. An interval is **HARMONIC** if the notes are
    written **BESIDE** each other, played separately: ☐   ☑

8. This is a **DOTTED HALF NOTE**:   ☑   ☐

9. This time signature tells us that there are
    four counts in each measure: $\frac{4}{4}$ ☑   ☐

10. 𝑝 tells us to play **LOUDLY**.   ☐   ☑

11. 𝑓 tells us to play **SOFTLY**.   ☐   ☑

12. To be able to play the piano well, you only need
    to practice **THREE DAYS** each week.   ☐ ✓   ☐

CORRESPONDS WITH PAGES 44 AND 45 OF BEANSTALK'S LESSON PREP B.

REVIEW

1. Write the following whole notes on the staff.

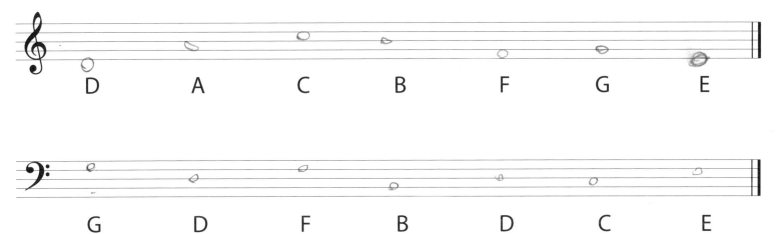

D   A   C   B   F   G   E

G   D   F   B   D   C   E

2. Name the following notes.

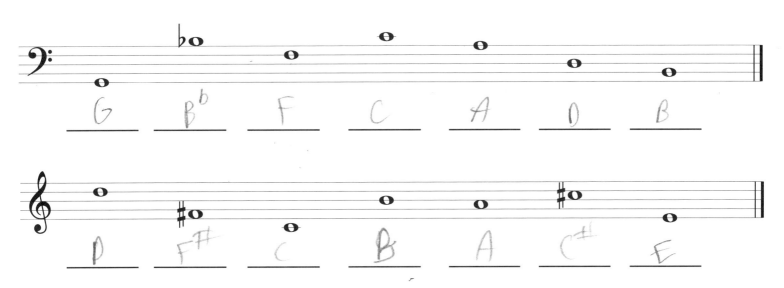

G   B♭   F   C   A   D   B

D   F#   C   B   A   C#   E

3. Draw a **TREBLE CLEF** sign.

4. Draw a **BASS CLEF** sign.

CORRESPONDS WITH PAGES 46 AND 47 OF BEANSTALK'S LESSON PREP B.

5. Write the **COUNTS** for the following measures.

1 2 3 4   1 2 3 4   1 2 3 4   1 2 3 4

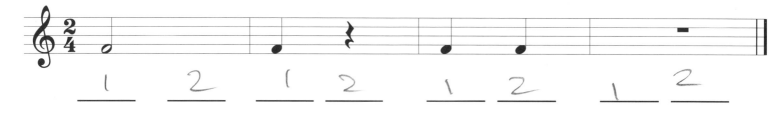

1 2   1 2   1 2   1 2

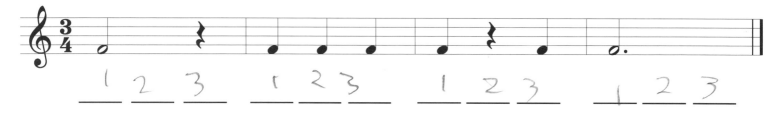

1 2 3   1 2 3   1 2 3   1 2 3

6. Draw a **SHARP** sign. _____

7. Draw a **FLAT** sign. _____

8. Draw a **NATURAL** sign. _____

9. Draw a **CRESCENDO** sign. _____

10. Draw a **DECRESCENDO** sign. _____

NOW HEAR THIS!

1. Your teacher will play a series of **3rds** twice. Close your eyes and listen. Are the **3rds HIGHER** or **LOWER**?

2. Your teacher will play a series of notes twice. Close your eyes and listen. Are the notes you are hearing played **LEGATO** or **STACCATO**?

FOR THE TEACHER:

1.

2.

CORRESPONDS WITH PAGES 46 AND 47 OF BEANSTALK'S LESSON PREP B.

12297